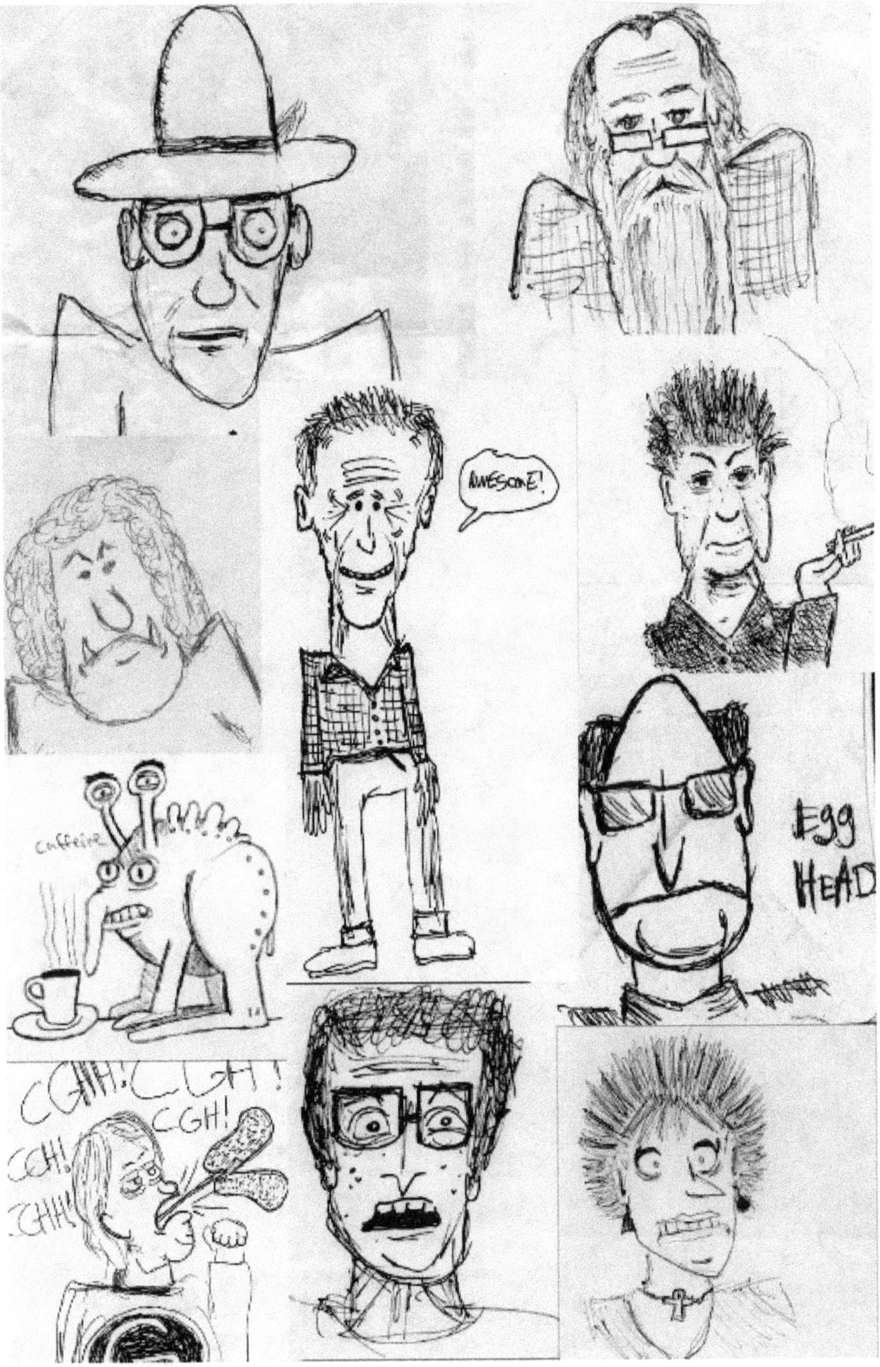

# Brady Street Pharmacy
## Stories and Sketches

## Tea Krulos

"You got to write about this place," Mo said.
"But no one will ever believe this shit."

-- Dedicated in memory to Maureen Jamieson aka "Mo"

**Table of Contents**

1. Zorro is Dead  
   7
2. The Magical Mystery Tour of Brady Street  
   11
3. Ode to Mo  
   15
4. Honey of a Hornet  
   22
5. Betting on Hockey  
   24
6. Three Weeks Without Shh-wedded Wheat  
   27
7. A Christmas Village of His Own  
   34
8. Dishwasher Saints  
   38
9. The 2600 Block of Pierce Street  
   43
10. Red Trips Da Light Fantastic  
    46
11. Watt-ever  
    51
12. Opening Night  
    56
13. You Can't Fight City Hall (but City Hall Might Stop by for Popcorn)  
    58
14. Anvil Chorus  
    62
15. Note to Mo  
    66
16. Lights Out  
    68

**Zorro is Dead**

When I met Jim, owner of the Brady Street Pharmacy—a classic greasy spoon diner: soda fountain, convenience store, pharmacy counter (and later also a performing arts space)—he was crying.

At that time, I was about 22 years old and had just quit a long series of shitty jobs—telemarketing, dishwashing, pulling weeds as a landscaper, and a bunch of temp jobs. Most recently on my resume I had been enjoying being carefree and unemployed. But now I had to come up with rent, damnit, and maybe a bag of groceries and a bottle of cheap booze. I wandered the East Side of Milwaukee filling out job applications, growing sick of writing my own name.

I walked into the Brady Street Pharmacy and scanned the contents of the building—rows of fluorescent lights and metal shelves set up as aisles. I approached a cash register near the entrance. It was set up like an island, a square counter with a small opening for the employees to walk in. On the back counter were a pile of boxes, the front had a cashier ringing a customer up, racks of cigarettes behind them. The cashier raised an eyebrow when I inquired about a job and pointed me to the other end of the store, where blue letters from the 1980s spelled out PRESCRIPTIONS. I walked down an aisle towards the letters.

The diner was on one side of a border of waist high magazine racks, which held hundreds of magazines, newspapers, romance paperbacks, and coloring books. The diner was full of East Side characters and my eyes grew big as I watched the waitresses balancing plates of hamburgers and meat loaf on their arms, swooping over half empty coffee cups with a pot—black spout for regular, orange for decaf—to fill them up. These waitresses were pros. I instantly identified several patrons as being obvious weirdos. This was before the smoking ban, so the air was filled with thick, blueish-grey secondhand smoke.

*Wow, this is like a David Lynch movie!* I gleefully thought. It certainly had enough pies and coffee cups to act as props. I was to find that some days the Pharmacy was as profoundly human as Edward Hopper's painting *Nighthawks*, other days it was as ugly and brutal as something written by Charles Bukowski.

My eyes looked down at the magazines passing by me—*Time*, *People*, *TV Guide*, *Weekly World News*, *GQ*, *Milwaukee Magazine*,*Varmint Hunter*, *Royal Life Magazine*, the *Daily Racing Form*, on and on. I turned and looked the other direction—rack after rack filled with bright primary color candy packaging, every sugary sweet of your dreams.

I reached the pharmacy counter. No one appeared to be there. I looked around. From where I was, you could see into the kitchen, where there were a couple of cooks and a dishwasher. They didn't seem too busy.

A portly cook, covered in grease, saw me looking at them.

"HEY, JIM!" He yelled. "CUSTOMER!"

A mousy man with bright white hair, a bland yellow dress shirt, and a tie with King Kong swatting at airplanes from the Empire State Building on it, stood up from somewhere behind the pharmacy counter. His eyes were red, and he wiped them with his hand.

"I'm sorry, just kind of a rough day here," Jim said, sadly. He shrugged his shoulders and lifted his hands up. "Zorro died." He said this as if I would understand completely.

"Oh?" I replied, confused. "Umm...Zorro? Like the actor who played him?" Jim must have realized then that I had never met him before.

"My bird." He pointed to something behind me, and I turned to see an empty birdcage hanging from the ceiling by a white plastic chain. I hadn't noticed it on my walk back to the pharmacy counter because I had been gawking the other direction at the cafe full of eccentric characters.

"A canary. He died today."

I looked at the cigarette smoke drifting through the building. Perhaps Zorro was the canary in the coal mine.

"I'm sorry to hear that," I said. Jim crossed his arms and stared straight ahead at the empty birdcage, nodding slightly. A few seconds passed.

"So I—" I began.

"Yes!"
"I was wondering if I could fill out a job application?"

Jim scrambled some papers around on his desk, licked a finger then pulled one up and slapped it on the pharmacy counter.

"Done!" He said, one of his favorite words of punctuation. I sat down in the diner and filled it out while the waitresses—three no nonsense, middle aged, career waitresses—eyed me suspiciously. One of them casually walked by me with a pot of coffee, hoping to look over my shoulder and glean some information.

I finished the application and brought it back to the pharmacy counter. Jim was on the phone.

"No. No. No....done!" He said to someone and hung up. Then he grabbed my application.

"Ok, we're rockin' and rollin," he said as he walked away with my application, without further comment.

The next day I got a call from Jim.

"Hiya, how about starting tomorrow, 11AM?"

"Ok, sure," I replied, I mean what else did I have to do? It looked like I'd be making rent next month. Good stuff.

"Roger that, over and out," Jim said, hanging up the phone.

I figured I'd do as I usually did and work this job as a dishwasher (and then a cashier) for a few months, pay some rent, buy a few bags of groceries, maybe even some new socks, save a tiny bit, and then quit. Such was my life.

I worked there for ten years.

**The Magical Mystery Tour of Brady Street**

The Brady Street Pharmacy was located on the west end of Brady Street, near the intersection of Humboldt Boulevard, where Saint Hedwig's church stands.

West of this intersection, in Saint Hedwig's shadow, was the Italian part of Brady Street. The Pharmacy was surrounded by other businesses on the block that ended with an Italian *O*—there was Sciortino's, a bakery that filled the neighborhood with the delicious smell of freshly baked bread and advertised a hot ham and rolls Sunday special on a hand-painted sign; Fazio's, a small dry cleaner and tailor business run by Josephine, who would sit in a chair behind the counter and watch soap operas on a small TV while waiting for customers; on the corner was Regano's Roman Coin, a classic neighborhood tavern that had been there for over a hundred years, and Glorioso's, the best Italian grocery store and deli in the city. I would squeeze through the narrow aisles of Glorioso's and stop at the deli for pasta salad or a meatball or caprese sandwich sometimes at lunch. There was briefly an Italian souvenir store just off Brady on Humboldt that celebrated the ethnicity of the neighborhood and sold Italian flags and novelty shirts that said things like "I'M NOT YELLING, I'M ITALIAN."

Every morning, there was an assembly of old Italian men who gathered for breakfast in the Pharmacy. They began to arrive as soon as the doors opened at 8am and slowly drifted in over the next hour until there were 10-15 of them taking up a few tables along the windows. They were known collectively as "The Italians." They chatted in a mix of English and Italian, and pretty frequently the discussion would be heated. They would begin to yell and use aggressive hand gestures, occasionally one of them would pound the table, clattering coffee cups on saucers and rattling the silverware. Every so often, one of them would storm out of the cafe in an angry huff, red-faced and swearing loudly. But they would be back the next morning.

I don't speak Italian, so I didn't know what they were so passionately arguing about, but sometimes curiosity would get the better of me and I'd ask one of them as I rang them up at the cash register, "what was that guy's deal?"

"Ah, Mario," would be the answer, a hand waved dismissively, "he's all bent outta shape about politics." These "politics" ranged from international and national down to Milwaukee city politics and even smaller to the microcosm of the Italian Community Center, a space in Milwaukee's Third Ward and the heart of Italian-Milwaukee culture. This is where things like Festa Italiana, a big summer festival celebrating Italian culture, are planned and passions run high about these things.

In the late afternoon, a younger group of Italians would come in, young guys that had moved here from Italy that had married into Italian-American families. They'd stop in with their wives and kids to have social time together.

East of Humboldt, Brady Street was a little hipper. In the 1960s and 70s Brady Street was the heart of Milwaukee's counterculture, and the area was heavily populated by hippies. There were headshops that sold drug paraphernalia, psychedelic posters, Jefferson Airplane records, and underground comix. Weed was openly smoked on the streets, and Brady Street was labelled the "Haight-Ashbury of Milwaukee," comparing it to the famous hippie district of San Francisco. Some of these hippies never moved on, and the Pharmacy had quite a few longhairs gone grey as regulars. Every evening, a group of artists and free thinkers that called themselves "The Gang" gathered around 6pm for dinner. In the 70s they had been rock musicians, underground newspaper editors, and protest organizers, but now they worked their day jobs, had social time with each other remembering glory days and enjoying a slice of pie each evening before heading home for the day.

A younger group of college-age people hung around Brady, too. These people were more hip than hippie (though a few of them dressed like they stepped right out of the 1960s) and frequented places on the east end of the street like the Hi-Hat Lounge, the Nomad, Up & Under Pub, and Thurman's 15. Brady Street, like many other avenues in Milwaukee, sure knows how to toss back the drinks.

All of these people—the groups of Italians that lived on the Lower Eastside, the Boomers still in love with Brady Street, the hungover college kids looking for something greasy to eat, the people who wanted to give their money to a small business instead of a corporate box store, and all those seeking refuge from the harsh outside world with a cup of coffee and a cheap plate of food—they formed the microcosm that kept the Pharmacy in business for 26 years.

Being there was one of the first times in my life that I felt like I was part of a neighborhood. Up until that point, my entire social life was my bubble of friends. They were mostly my age, punk rockers and artistic types. But being a cashier, I had to be social and talk to all sorts of people, whether I wanted to or not—the Italians who worked at all the neighboring businesses, the mailman who would get a coffee to go and talk to me for a few minutes before carrying on with his route, the beat cops on the trail of some shoplifter, the nuns who stopped in for their medications, the newspaper delivery guy who would tell me about how he had spent 36 hours straight playing World of Warcraft over the weekend. Reflecting the greater disparity of the eastside area in general, there were guest appearances by politicians running for office looking to shake hands and kiss babies, and homeless people wanting to scrape together a dollar.

I got to know many of the regulars to varying degrees. There was a mysterious middle-aged woman in a bright purple beret and matching lipstick and floral print coat who obviously had a large number of cats—she stopped in every other day for cat food and litter, but never said more than "please" or "thank you."

There were less mysterious regulars like Auggie, who talked away about any and every detail of his life. A former train conductor, Auggie would waddle in like a penguin in a bright red suit coat and fur lined bomber's hat, sometimes pulling out a brass-colored pocket watch to check the time. He was eccentric and drove some of the waitresses crazy, but I grew to like him. He'd clip out comic strips from the newspaper he thought were funny and give them to me; one year during the holidays he gave me one of my favorite Christmas gifts—fruit shaped magnets from the Dollar Store, which decorated my refrigerator for years until they fell apart.

Auggie, like many of the regulars, was suffering from one of the most terrible human afflictions—loneliness. I talked to people about anything and everything, from the most useless small talk to some of the darkest confessions I have ever heard. I credit that contact with a wide spectrum of people, not just those who looked like me and liked the same things, as helping me develop as a person and as a writer.

Welcome to the human race, kid.

## Ode to Mo

"Hey, new guy! I need your help, honey," were the first words Mo said to me. She was leaning on the counter by the kitchen, a long white cigarette dangling out of her mouth. She had thin, short grey hair and cat-like eyes peering at me through bifocals. She was wearing a flannel over our work uniform, which at that time was a blue medical scrub shirt.

"Ok," I said. I put down a bus pan of dirty dishes and followed her to a back hallway where there were stacks of 12 packs of soda on a dull grey cart, a cart I was to use thousands of times over the next decade.

"All this fucking soda has to go upstairs. Follow me," she groaned, grabbed a 12-pack in each hand, grunted the word "fuck," and started up the stairs. I loaded four or five 12-packs into my gangly arms. Mo turned around.

"Don't be a fucking show off," she said out of the corner of her mouth, cigarette still dangling, eyeing all the cases in my arms. She snorted out a laugh. These were the first things I learned about Mo: she loved to chain-smoke cigarettes, pop pills, and she could swear a sailor under a table.

My favorite thing about Mo was when she was about to go on a particularly profane tirade to one of her friends visiting her at work, she'd turn to me and say, "cover your ears, hon." I tried telling her I had witnessed the works of John Waters and GG Allin, and could handle her colorful language, but she just pinched my cheek and told me to "shut the fuck up."

We got to the top of the stairs with our 12-packs, where there was a huge storage room, with shelves and pallets full of canned food, cases of potato chips, stacks of soda and beer, and supplies for the cafe. But what caught my eye was a woman with long, greasy hair sitting on a crate, talking to herself as she cut a coupon from a newspaper. There was a stack of newspapers a couple feet high next to her and in front of her on another crate was a messy pile of coupons. She had on glasses—the kind that shade over in the sunlight but always have a brownish tint on the lenses—and a bleach stained, well-worn Green Bay Packers shirt.

When me and Mo entered the room, she made no acknowledgement of our presence and continued to mumble to herself, carefully clipping a coupon with a hefty silver scissors. Mo looked at me, puffed smoke and rolled her eyes, as if that was all the explanation I needed for the woman's presence. Later I'd find out she was Jim's deceased wife's sister, who ran errands for Jim in exchange for an endless supply of coupons and Diet Coke from the soda fountain.

We stacked our 12-packs, then headed downstairs. Mo grabbed another couple cases.

"I can finish hauling this upstairs, if you got other stuff to do," I told her, trying to be friendly.

"Please," she said, as if this suggestion was ridiculous, and slapped me on the arm. "Just cause I'm an old lady, don't mean I can't kick your ass," she said, laughing and leaning around the corner into the kitchen, where she had stashed an ashtray under the hand washing sink. She stubbed her cigarette out.

"My name is Maureen, by the way," she told me. "But everyone calls me Mo."

##

Me and Mo were best work buddies, and we were there for each other. Every Friday I carried her grocery bags—soda, cartons of cigarettes, gossip magazines, cat litter, Hamburger Helper, Campbell's soup—to her house. She rented a lower flat that was two blocks away from the Pharmacy.

Mo helped me with morale often, but the moment I remember most was when me and my wife split up, heading for divorce. I knew something bad was happening and then she was just gone one day. It was pretty rough. I was scheduled to work and that morning was the most awful thing I've woken up to. It was a cold spring day and I trudged to work. I was late.

Mo inhaled from her cigarette slowly as she watched me walk in. I guess she could read everything on my face. She exhaled smoke all over me as she gave me a hug.

"Go home," she said softly.

"But I—"

"Uh *duh duh duh*, no," Mo said, making the sound effect she made when she was telling you not to argue with her. "Take the day off. We got it covered."

I walked home very slowly. I stopped at the grocery store's liquor department on the way and got a single item—a bottle of rum, wrapped in a brown paper bag. I continued my journey, but was in no rush to get there. My friend Coth appeared at the end of my block, weaving back and forth on his bicycle.

"How's it going, man?" He asked as I approached. I couldn't lie and said, "Ok."

"Not so great. Me and my wife split up," I said, casting my eyes toward the ground.

"Oh shit! Shit, what are you going to do?"

"Well, first I'm going to drink this entire bottle of rum," I told him, holding up the bottle. "After that, I got no idea."

I walked away as he called out, "good luck," after me.

I drank that bottle of rum and things were hard, and the healing was a long process, but things got better. Mo helped me out along the way, checking in, making sure I was eating, and convincing a young lawyer who came in for lunch every day to help me with divorce paperwork *pro bono* (Jason Cleereman, who later tragically died as a victim of a road rage incident).

Mo talked a tough game and she had a lot of rough spots throughout her life. But she had a heart of gold.

##

There was one particular day with Mo I recall fondly. I made notes about it at the time. We were having a trying day with what we called the "wingnuts," the eccentric or sometimes just straight up crazy customers that frequented the Pharmacy. We had nicknames for these characters. Looking back at it, a lot of the nicknames were mean-spirited, but we were frustrated and exhausted and were trained to be cashiers, not mental health professionals. Talking shit about the customers is a service industry wide way of blowing off steam.

"Stand Up and Pee Lady," for example, got her name because she preferred to urinate standing above the toilet with the stall door open, muttering to herself. "Scammy Davis Jr" was an aggressive panhandler who slightly resembled the Rat Pack member. "Jeffrey Dahmer," we suspected, was a serial killer, so we named him after Milwaukee's most infamous former resident. "The Pirate" was a crabby old guy with a beard and an eye-patch. "The Cougher" was just a woman who smoked and coughed all the time.

Well, on this day, all of them came through—Stand Up and Pee Lady, Scammy Davis Jr., Jeffrey Dahmer, The Pirate, The Cougher, and many more.

"It's got to be a full moon or some shit," Mo rasped from behind a cloud of cigarette smoke, squinting and shaking her head.

We'd had to kick out a former regular who had gotten the nickname "Filthy McNasty" (Mo coined that one) who, as you might imagine, had some personal hygiene issues. He was also incredibly rude. He had this scraggly, long, salt and pepper hair, and a walrus moustache which, like his long, dirty fingernails, were stained yellow from cigarette smoke. He wore badly stained jeans and a t-shirt with holes in it, a bit too small so it exposed his hairy gut. He wore thick, smudged glasses, which he would push up the bridge of his nose with a long, yellow fingernail. He would come in and sit for hours, drinking coffee, chain-smoking, sometimes digging a newspaper out of the trash to read when he ordered the lunch special.

My terrible memory of Filthy McNasty is the day he decided to gorge himself on fudge. We would often put candy that didn't sell well on the counter at a discount to get rid of it, and this particular day we had a box of fudge squares for 59¢ each. McNasty came up to the counter to pay his bill—he had, as usual, been sitting in the cafe for hours, drinking a bottomless cup of coffee. He wiggled his gross fingernails and pointed one at the box of fudge squares.

"Gimme one a them fudges," he said. I rang him up for the coffee and candy, and he went over to a nearby chair, sat and wolfed it down. He licked his fingers, threw the wrapper in the garbage and returned to the counter.

"Gimme another one," he demanded, pointing at the fudge.

In total, he ate five fudge squares, one by one, paying for each individually, sitting down to scarf them in rapid succession. After the fifth fudge, however, there was a horrible gurgling sound that came out of his throat, Filthy McNasty shot up on his feet and bent over slightly as a puddle of regurgitated chocolate streamed out of his mouth and onto the carpeted floor below him. He looked at it a second, then turned and walked out the door without saying a word.

"Uhhhh….ah…." Is all I could think of to say as I shuddered and looked around to see if anyone else had witnessed the horrible spectacle.

Filthy McNasty got on the long list of People Banned from the Pharmacy, a rogue's gallery of shoplifters, perverts, waitress stalkers, serial check bouncers, drunken shit-talkers, and other wretches of society. He didn't get the ban for the fudge puke; I think it was for trying to steal cigars out of the humidor near the front counter.

And now, there he was "trying to weasel his way back in!" Mo said, looking up from a box full of packs of sanitary napkins she was slapping with a yellow pricing gun (the Pharmacy never upgraded to a scanner).

"Oh fuck no!" Mo said, exhaling a cloud of smoke, and setting down her pricing gun. I followed her lead, setting down my pricing gun next to the box of licorice packs I was pricing.

As Filthy McNasty began walking through the door, we both took a breath. Our techniques for kicking people out were different. Mo ranted and raved, swearing up a storm, making all sorts of threats—cops, bodily harm, talking to someone's mom at church, maybe all of the above. My style was "strong and silent." I would bounce up on the balls of my feet, making me close to seven feet tall, and I would just silently point at the person. It usually worked. People would make denials that were actually confessions of their crimes, and when they saw my pointing hand wasn't wavering, they would see themselves out.

So Filthy McNasty walked in. On one side of the counter, Mo was bellowing smoke and profane threats: "get the fuck out of here you fucking scumbag, you know you're not allowed in here you stupid shit, so turn your ass around immediately and fuck off…" while I stood at the other side of the counter, puffed up, silent, pointing right at him. Filthy McNasty scratched his exposed hairy gut with his long, yellow fingernails, muttering "bullshit, bullshit," until he couldn't take Mo's abuse anymore, turned on his heel and left.

Mo exhaled angrily, shook her head back and forth, walked behind the counter by me, grabbed her container filled with pills—which was actually a black plastic tube that used to hold a roll of Kodak camera film, threw back her head and swallowed a couple, then took a drink of Diet Coke from a Styrofoam cup.

"I swear to God, if I so much as see one more crazy person, I'm going to go find a gun, put it against my head," she said, pantomiming a gun with her hand, "and pull the goddamn trigger."

Right as she finished saying the sentence, we both looked out the window. A woman shuffled by, muttering to herself. She was carrying a big duffle bag shaped like a fish, my guess was that it was a pike or a muskie. I looked at Mo and raised an eyebrow.

"Well…" I said. Mo grabbed my arm and bit me through my shirt.

"Shut the fuck up," she yelled, and then she started laughing until tears were rolling down her face. Sometimes if you can't beat 'em, you have to go a little crazy and join 'em.

**Honey of a Hornet**

I started at the Pharmacy as a dishwasher (I was soon promoted to cashier). One day, I was walking around the lunch counter emptying overflowing ashtrays, dumping undrunk coffee, arranging and rearranging greasy plates and stacking them into a buspan.

I said hi to John as he came in, one of our regulars. John was elderly, his face heavily lined, wrinkled, big, rubbery ears and nose. White hair stuck out from underneath his U.S. Navy baseball cap, a gold logo on a black hat. He wore that every day, along with a light tan jacket. He had cloudy cataracts in one eye, so his vision wasn't great, but his routine was so consistent he could probably walk through it with his eyes shut.

John came in to have something to do, and because of the waitresses. They were kind to him, listened to his old man stories, made sure his cup of decaf was always full. He liked to watch their bodies move around and think of his glory days. He'd strike up polite conversation with anyone near him, about whatever—sports, politics, weather, the Pharmacy's lunch specials.

On this day, a man sat at the counter next to John and ordered hot water and a packet of honey. He was unkempt and there was a wild look in his eyes.

"That's it? Hot water and a packet of honey?" the waitress asked him, her voice dripping with disgust and aggravation.

The man didn't notice the waitress's irritation and nodded at her slowly. She returned with a little blue plastic pot filled with hot water poured from a spigot on the coffee machine, an empty coffee cup, and a packet of honey. She set it all down with a loud sigh. The man smiled slightly. He took the honey packet between his thumb and pointer finger and flipped it back and forth. He turned to John.

"Hey man, guess what? I can tell whether honey comes from a bee, a wasp, or a hornet just by tasting it," the stranger told John.

"Izzata fact?" John grunted, looking out of the corner of his eye suspiciously at the man. I hung out by the counter nearby, stacking dishes and eavesdropping.

"Oh yes. Do you know how I know whether it comes from a bee, whether it comes from a hornet, or whether it comes from a wasp?"

"No."

"God tells me," the man said, smiling widely, as if this was the most wonderful thing.

"Izzata fact?" John replied. Then they sat in silence, John sipping his coffee, his hungry good eye following the waitresses' bodies as they darted around loading their arms with plates of food, grabbing coffee pots, while his mysterious neighbor sipped his hot water and honey.

The man kept the honey's origin a secret, and no one asked.

**Betting on Hockey**

One of the regulars for the diner was a man named Pete. He came in almost every evening. He was recovering from an addiction, I would find out after years of talking to him, and having a routine was a way to work through it. Pete was a big Italian guy who was always trying to catch his breath—he could make it about 10 steps before he would need to stop and gasp for air, his shark-like face huffing and puffing. He had grey-colored skin, a brown leather jacket like the Fonz, and a sharp widow's peak, his hair dyed jet black. He looked like a cross between a character on *The Sopranos* and a vampire.

He would sit and drink coffee, cup after cup, and sometimes order food. Often, he'd be joined by his father, Louie, a small, wrinkled man with wispy grey hair slicked back on his head and a newsie cap, usually chewing on a toothpick. One day, though, Louie walked back into the kitchen and yelled at a cook about how his eggs had been cooked out and got kicked out. Other neighborhood characters would join Pete sometimes and they would chat about the day's news and gossip and try to flirt with the waitresses.

Afterward, Pete would pay his $1.75 for the coffee at the cash register, catch his breath, and talk to me for a few minutes—it was usually small talk: the weather, sports, stuff like that. He would stand there with hands on the counter, leaning on it and breathing heavily between sentences.

One night he decided that instead of talking about the meatloaf ("it was good") or the unrelenting rain, he wanted to confess to me about the terrible gambling addiction he used to have. Service industry people hear more confessions than Catholic priests.

Pete's gambling problem ruined his life at the time. His wife left him over it and he "owed money to people you don't want to owe money to," he said, shaking his head in shame. "You know who I'm talking about?"

I nodded my head and said "I think so." I was kind of afraid to ask more, but I knew the East Side was where the head of the Milwaukee Mafia had once lived.

Pete started on horses, flipping through the *Daily Racing Form*, and he'd bet on the Super Bowl—no big deal. But after a while he was betting on every football, baseball, and basketball game, every horse race, dog race, and car race. He often lost, but when he won...wow, what a feeling! He wanted more, but he was running out of things to bet on, so he turned to golf, tennis...and hockey.

"Let me tell you, that's when you know you got a goddamn problem, when you start betting on hockey games," Pete told me, exhaling and then taking a big gasp of air as he laughed. I imagined Pete in a corner bar on Brady Street, a haze of cigarette smoke floating across a TV above a bar. He's convinced the bartender to tune into an NHL game and Pete is gripping an old fashioned in despair, muttering profanities as a hotshot forward slaps a puck past the goalie and sinks a stack of Pete's cash along with it.

Pete finally admitted he had a problem. He threw the *Daily Racing Form* in the trash and stopped betting on hockey games. He stopped going to the corner bar where all his cronies were waiting to make a bet. He went to work, and when done, he started heading straight to the Pharmacy to get a cup of coffee and maybe the meatloaf if he was hungry. He hung out with his dad and a few friends from the neighborhood. He made corny jokes to the waitresses so he could see them smile. He talked to Yours Truly about the weather. Then he went home to watch some TV and go to sleep.

Yes, it's boring and repetitive. But at least he no longers owes money to people you don't want to owe money to.

**Three Weeks Without Shh-wedded Wheat**

Not every day, but often when I worked, I would plunk down fifty cents for the day's copy of the *Milwaukee Journal Sentinel*. I usually worked a shift from noon until 8pm, the parameters became looser as the years went on. I usually also worked the morning opening shift Saturday or Sunday or both. Between lunch and dinner, the afternoon was usually slow. That's when I did a lot of stocking and cleaning. But Jim would often be asleep at his desk during the afternoon, so it was also when the employees slacked off. I would get the paper, wail and gnash my teeth about the day's headlines—I worked at the Pharmacy for the entirety of the George W. Bush presidency, so there was plenty of bad news. I sometimes would read the lighter news like Dear Abby, or roll my eyes at some comic strips.

I treated my fifty-cent purchase like a hunter determined to use every piece of the animal they had killed, none going to waste—I gave the sports section to the guys in the kitchen. The coupons were given to Mo and she would take what she wanted and pass the rest on to her friends. After I read the news, I'd pass it on to the waitstaff or customers who came in for the dinner shift. I gave it all away, except the crossword puzzle.

I would carefully fold the paper backwards, then fold it again, so it wasn't much bigger than the puzzle itself, then I'd set it on the cigarette racks behind the register and slowly knock it out in between customers, writing the answers in all caps with a black pen.

Number 1 across. *Six pack?*—*ABS*. 45 down. *Director Craven*—*WES*. Start with the easy ones.

People were creatures of habit—they stopped in to get their cigarettes and gallon of milk, or to eat a cheap burger while they read the *Wall Street Journal*, or a hangover breakfast Saturday morning. People had their brand of cigarette or soda, a favorite magazine or candy bar, and no substitute would do.

Reading my stories, you might have the impression that everyone that entered the Pharmacy was butt ugly. While it's true there was a high concentration of beautifully repugnant people, there were all types that hung out there—young, old, all races, creeds, and economic backgrounds.

35 across. *Mid-month date—IDES*. 8 down. *Syrian city—ALEPPO*.

I developed a little crush on a gal my age who stopped in for coffee in the afternoon every couple days. She came in alone and sat in the same spot at a table directly in my eyeline from the counter. She would sit down, smile at the waitress, order a coffee, then open a book and start reading. She had tattoos of geometric shapes on her arms. She was a little weird looking, and by that, I mean attractive. I would stand and look at my crossword puzzle, but I'd let my eyes drift up slightly to look at her, sipping coffee and reading.

I wanted to talk to her, but what could I possibly say to her that would be interesting?

My other problem was that I was stuck on 25 across. 15 across was *London airport—HEATHROW*. 42 across, *crowded with vegetation—OVERGROW*, there's the theme for the longer words, words that end with ROW. But what the hell was 25 across? "Ragtime author." Something-ROW.

Was I interesting?

*AHAB. COAT. IDLE.*

Not really.

*BOIL. RUDE. ISLE.*

She brought her check up to the counter to pay. Here was my chance.

"How's it going?" I asked.

"Oh good," she said, smiling brightly. "Yeah, how are things going here?"

"Good, real good."

"That's good. Well, see you later."

I sighed, irritated with myself. Great talk, champ. I turned around and discovered Mo was hovering over my crossword puzzle, squinting at it through the cigarette smoke billowing out of her face. She grabbed a pen and handed it to me.

"DOCTOROW. I saw you were stuck on 25 across. Trust me, I've been doing crosswords for a hundred years."

A couple weeks later, conversations between me and the crush were slightly less awkward. One day, I was chatting her up when I saw a small blur in the corner of my eye. I ignored it as I was enraptured in conversation. But then I heard a shrill screech:

"EXCUSE ME!" Slowly, I turned. There was a petite old woman standing at the end of the counter. She had on a drab, dark green dress with a collar that looked like a doily and a matching hat. The hat looked like a green velvet bucket with a large bright green and yellow fabric flower attached to the hatband. Her eyes were magnified like an owl behind thick lenses.

"Yesssssss?" I hissed, annoyed that my flirting had been interrupted.

"FOLLOW ME. I WANT TO SHOW YOU SOMETHING." I looked at my crush and shrugged. "Looks like you're busy," she smirked and waved good-bye. Irritation spread over me, and I turned to follow the little old lady into the maze of aisles of shelves. She moved very slowly, her gnarled hand pushing her cane like someone would push an oar. I shuffled as slowly as I could behind her, moving my feet centimeter by centimeter.

"HERE," she said, lifting an accusing finger to an empty spot on the shelf by the Apple Jacks and Cocoa Puffs. I looked at the spot, then looked back at her, raising an eyebrow.

"WELL?!"

"Well, what?" I asked. "What's supposed to be here?"

"WHAT?!"

"What's supposed to be here?!" I asked, louder. She made a disgusted, clucking sound.

"The SHH-WEDDED WHEAT, OF COURSE! WHEN WILL YOU GET MORE SHH-WEDDED WHEAT IN?"

I paused a second. Her pronunciation of "Shredded" threw me off. I thought for a second—is that how it's pronounced? Had I been wrong all these years?

"Well, not until—"

"MY GOD HOW TALL ARE YOU?" She said, cutting me off. I shook my head.

"No." I said. I am quite tall and at that age, talking about it annoyed me.

"HOW TALL?"

"OK, well I'm about six—"

"WHEN WILL YOU GET MORE SHH-WEDDED WHEAT IN? WHEN? WHAT DAY?"

I took a deep breath. I was losing my temper with this little old lady. I thought about when we would get the next delivery of groceries. A truck would pull up by the alley door of the building and two delivery drivers would load up handcarts and fill the back hallway with stacks of boxes.

"Uh, Tuesday." I said, trying not to look directly at her.

"WHAT?!"

"TUESDAY!" I shouted. A couple of customers browsing combs nearby turned to look.

"Tuesday, Tuesday," the woman muttered as she walked away. "Tuesday."

She wandered around the store and every time she saw something she needed on the shelf she'd yell "HELP! HELP!" until I came over, got the item and placed it on the counter. Then there was the slow counting out of worn dollar bills and coins, the double-bagging, calling a taxi and instructing the driver to come inside and help her with her groceries. All while a long line formed behind her giving me the stink eye for the hold up.

*Good. God.* I thought as the woman walked away. But my ass wasn't out of the fire yet.

The woman returned on Tuesday, but the Shh-wedded, er Shredded Wheat, had not sailed in to dock with the rest of the groceries. I was called a "LIAR," questioned loudly and extensively until I called back from the cash register to the pharmacy desk. I didn't have a chance to talk to the cute girl at all, she just waved with her fingertips as she walked by and out the front door.

"Jim, you got to help me out. This woman is demanding we get her some Shredded Wheat. ASAP," I said. The phone call was really performance art for the woman, who couldn't hear well enough to pick up the conversation but was standing there staring me down as I talked on the phone.

"10-4. Done!" Jim said, but if I really needed the job done, I knew I'd need to talk to Mo—Jim had the memory of a gnat.

"Mo, this woman is going to murder me over this Shredded Wheat. Must be good stuff, I never tried it. Please order some. As many boxes as they'll send," I pleaded. Mo laughed and blew smoke out her nose.

"Look out for those old ladies, they'll fuck you up!"

Mo saved me again, here. The Shredded Wheat came in the following Tuesday. I hid the boxes behind the counter in the off chance someone would stop in and buy them all before the woman came in. I needed this Shredded Wheat situation to be over.

The woman came in and began walking by me. I grabbed one of the boxes of cereal and leaned on the counter in front of me. "Heyyyy! Hey, excuse me. EXCUSE ME! Look what I got!" The woman turned to look at me. She squinted. She didn't smile, her eyes didn't light up, she just shuffled forward and grabbed the box out of my hand.

"I HAVEN'T HAD SHH-WEDDED WHEAT FOR THREE WEEKS! THREE WEEKS BECAUSE OF YOU!" She began to shuffle off to find more items so she could yell "HELP! HELP!" until I came and grabbed them between customers. I sighed—ah well, at least it's over. But then she stopped and turned around.

"THANK YOU." She said, hugging the box of Shredded Wheat—almost as big as her torso, before turning back around to her shopping.

Years later I had a job interview. More service industry stuff. The manager asked, "Can you give me an example of a time you went above and beyond to help a customer out?" I really hate that question—*hmm, how about all the times I didn't actually murder a customer?* I thought. But instead, I said, "Yes. I was working at this place called the Pharmacy. There was this little lady. She very badly wanted me to get her some Shh-wedded...uh, excuse me, *Shredded* Wheat and we happened to be out..."

**A Christmas Village of His Own**

Jim's favorite holiday tradition was setting up his model Christmas Village, which spread about 30 feet along the windows of the entire length of the diner. Each window had its own little scene, but they all connected into the most Christmassy community ever. It was an all-day project setting the village up. When the inspiration struck him that it was Time-to-Set-Up-the-Village-Day, Jim would have the staff help him carry the boxes full of the entire townhood down the building's rickety wooden stairs from the attic storage loft, but after that, the project of assembly was all his.

Jim's deceased wife Barb was the one who started the collection. It was part of her annual shopping—she would pick up new decorations for the Pharmacy and additions to the Christmas Village, a new little ceramic building, or some miniature carolers. But she was gone now, and Jim almost never left the building. He lived upstairs and ate all his meals from the diner, grabbing candy bars out of the aisle for a snack. Sometimes he wouldn't leave the building for months. The expansion of the village had stopped, but there was enough for a full display.

After unwrapping all the pieces from old, crumpled newspaper, he would climb in between the customers trying to eat their lunch into the big windowsills of the diner to first lay down sheets of snowy white fabric, then fussed around with buildings and miniature street signs and groups of little figures until they looked exactly right.

In the evening, after the customers left, Jim would wait until the dishwasher finished mopping the floors, then he'd stand in the empty cafe, sipping a Styrofoam cup full of lukewarm coffee. He'd stare deep into his Christmas Village, happiness flooding over him.

Look at this beautiful world! As charming as a Norman Rockwell painting—none of the graffiti and litter or aggressive panhandling drug addicts of Brady Street, not a stack of unpaid bills anywhere in sight, just people filled with holiday joy. There they were handing each other gifts wrapped in crisp, bright colors—the paint was still bright on the ceramic figures after all of these years.

Over here, in the first window, that's where these citizens began their shopping list, in the cozy nook of Speciality Shops. This town lived back in the good old days, whenever that was, before Wal-Mart and fast-food empires had bulldozed our culture. When the village supported the mom and pop shop instead of some soulless warehouse full of junk.

There was Dicken's Bookshop, a compact little red brick building with a display of little green and red hardcovers in the window, a wreath hanging on the door, a yellow light illuminating the windows, the promise of warm winter reading inside. Next to it was the Joys of Toys store, nice wooden toys on display in the window. And the Bakery! Jim could practically smell the warm bread inside, and everyone's favorite, the Candy Shoppe with giant peppermint candy cane posts outside as decorations. Inside there were enough sweet treats to fill everyone's stockings.

Jim's eyes followed a couple walking close together, bundled up, with tiny ceramic cups in their hands. He sighed with longing. They had obviously just left Miss Kettle's Teashop & Cafe, perhaps heading into the next windowsill towards Smith's Curio Shoppe, right next door to the snow-covered offices of *The Gazette*. Notice how there is no name of a town or village in the paper's name? It's not the *Thiensville Gazette* or the *Cedarburg Gazette* because there is nowhere else outside of this village, a true microcosm. The one and only *Gazette*, between Smith's Curio Shoppe and the Slalom Home Ski shop, just down the street from the butcher, the baker, and the candlestick maker.

Jim continued his winter trek. There was the village train station, where a couple of elegant women in long coats, earmuffs, scarves, and mittens chatted next to...wait, *what the hell was this*? A yellow rubber triceratops was standing next to the ladies, as if participating in the conversation. Jim stared at it for a second, confused. Ah, must have been those dumb jokers in the kitchen. Always some goofy prank with those guys. He picked the triceratops out of his village and threw it at a nearby garbage bin, but it bounced off the side and went tumbling across the cafe floor and under the soda machine. Jim turned back to his triceratops-free village.

There, skating on a blue piece of plastic, was a group of merry ice skaters. Set up on the edge of the pond was a hot cocoa stand. A red pickup truck drove by, the driver waving at the ice skaters. A couple of the kiddos were having a snowball fight in the background. The truck bed held a snowy Christmas tree, so big it needed to be tied down. That's a good one, will look nice in the living room—that's probably his house right over there, Jim reasoned, following the path of his truck in his mind. I mean, that's the direction he's heading, to a row of nice wood and brick townhouses, lit up with Christmas lights and wreaths and boughs of holly.

And here, in the next window, the *pièce de résistance*—Town Square. Here was a charming, small town government—a little post office, with a kid dropping something in the mailbox outside—probably a letter to Santa, the lovable scamp! And the barbershop, where the real political discussions take place. Lampposts, each with a ceramic wreath hung on them, and pine trees line the path to City Hall, and the church, a steeple with a bell tower on top, which rings out noon and 6pm every day.

Look out front! Carolers! When did you see carolers anymore? Jim leaned forward, stooping down to get a closer look at them. And see, two of the carolers were black. This village was progressive. We weren't racists here in the Christmas Village, just folks that loved small town living.

*It's the most! wonderful! time of the year!* Jim hummed to himself, smiling, teary eyed, his mind a flood looking at the details of this happy place.

He soaked in every small detail and ignored the car outside the Pharmacy window that had been plowed in and was stuck in the snow, turning side to side, the wheel spinning, kicking up dirty, exhaust-colored snow and frozen litter into the air. That sort of thing wasn't a problem here in Christmas Village.

There, look who was leading the carolers in song, that little figure, the one with his arms outstretched, wearing a suit coat with tails, a top hat, and a sash wrapped around his torso that reads MAYOR. That could be him! Mayor Jim, benevolent and fun leader of this Christmas wonderland. He concentrated so hard on this that he could feel himself shrinking down into the village, his clothes transforming to the mayor's suitcoat, sash, top hat. *The most wonderful time of the year!*

Jim faced his constituency. A marching band dressed like bright red nutcrackers appeared and began to get into formation. Ah, of course, a Christmas parade! Exactly what the village needed.

A brass baton appeared in his white gloved hand and he began waving it, spreading holiday cheer, smiling and waving to the villagers who had lined up for the spectacle, while a marching band behind him played "Good King Wenceslas." They marched over the stone bridge, over Kringle Creek. Jim's body stood transfixed, taking a sip from his styrofoam cup as he projected himself into the scene, leading the Christmas parade.

But what of this terror descending upon the parade, scurrying from the kitchen windowsill into the Christmas Village? Jim spit cold coffee back into his cup—cockroaches! Giant cockroaches! The parade disbursed and ran screaming in all directions and then disappeared from his mind and he coldly dumped back into this cruel world. He looked around at the empty cafe and Christmas Village spread across the windowsills. He frowned and looked back out the corner of his eye to the roaches creeping along into the Christmas Village.

He put down his coffee cup, lifted his glasses to his forehead, rubbed his eyes, then went back to the storage room to get a can of bug spray.

# Dishwasher Saints

There were three consecutive dishwashers at the Pharmacy who died of alcohol related conditions, all in a span of about a year and a half. All three were somewhere in their fifties, not young, but not too old. They just gave up on life and drank themselves to death, as people in Wisconsin sometimes are prone to do. Wisconsin is where people spend good weather drinking outside and bad weather drinking inside and celebrate success and mourn loss with a drink in their hand. These are the martyred Alcoholic Saints of the Brady Street Pharmacy:

**Saint Joseph**

Saint Joseph had thin, greasy hair combed over his scaly, pock-marked head. He had a vulgar looking mustache and was missing a tooth, most likely from falling off a barstool. He had the looks of a cartoon character up to no good.

I got along with the guy alright. He'd stop by the cash register when it was slow and complain about work, and I'd nod my head and not say anything. Sometimes it was obvious he'd already been hitting the bottle.

He was unpopular with the waitresses, which is a bad place for a dishwasher to be. Beware. A waitstaff will conspire silently, plot and wait patiently, and then sabotage your very soul if you piss them off.

Such was the case with Saint Joseph. As soon as he slouched through the door, you could see the back hair of the waitresses starting to stand on end, their postures clenched and uncomfortable. He came to work noticeably drunk or hungover and often snuck off to a side room to catch a few Zs. The servers were convinced he had a bottle hidden somewhere on the premises and they flipped the place more thoroughly than the Vice Squad. No stone was left unturned in the search for the stash in a desperate attempt to find hard alcohol evidence. One of the crew, Karen, even had me search the tank of the men's room toilet on a few occasions.

"Nothing but toilet water," I reported, shrugging.

Karen twitched with anger and irritation. "That son of a bitch is drinking, I know it—I can smell it on his breath!"

One day I walked in, and my co-worker Mo was smirking at me through a haze of cigarette smoke.

"Wait'll you see Saint Joe today." She said, exhaling smoke. "He's turned *yellow*."

"Sure, Mo." I said, dismissing it. I thought she was implying something like "he's a little green around the gills." Then he walked in.

"*He's....yellow!*" I whispered to Mo.

"I told you." She said.

"*No, no...he's yellow!*"

"I told you."

"*I mean, he looks like he walked out of an episode of The Simpsons!*" I'd never seen anything like it.

"I told you." Mo said again.

As you can probably guess, it's not a good sign when you turn as yellow as a yield sign. It means you are dying. And a few weeks later, Saint Joseph was dead.

### Saint Paul

Saint Paul had a drinking problem, too.

His doctor said "Saint Paul, if you continue to drink, you will drop over dead as a fucking doornail."

Saint Paul said, "Thanks for the advice, doc." Then he headed straight for the Roman Coin and bought a pitcher of beer and asked for one glass.

Saint Paul was a nice, jolly guy. He loved to laugh and joke around—usually. Sure, he was in a goddamn grouchy mood sometimes, but who isn't? I can't remember now if he quit or was fired for being drunk on the job, which happened on a regular basis. The booze made him happy. The waitresses were split on their decision on Paul. Most agreed he had "gotten worse."

Like I said, he was jolly. Jolly to me implies a little fat, which Paul was. He started to lose weight, rapidly, and it wasn't from dieting or exercise. The weight loss looked unnatural. His skin tone was changing, too, it was greenish-grayish. That's the best way I can describe it. It was like he was shriveling up and dying. It was depressing to see. I remember the last time I saw him, gray looking, soaking wet, walking in the rain with his XXL t-shirt hanging off his now L body, heading to the Roman Coin. Things got worse and he checked into the hospital. He didn't check out.


**Saint Pete**

It was kind of a surprise. I knew Saint Pete drank too much, and popped a lot of pain pills, which is a no no, but I didn't think much of it. He didn't look great, but he didn't look like he was going to drop over.

Peter had a bushy beard and long hair and a wild look in his eyes, like Rasputin. He was always dressed in the same beat-up flannel and jeans, chain smoking Old Golds. Initially the dude freaked me out a little bit, with all the staring and teeth grinding and mumbling to himself. Soon I realized that this was the pain pills talking and that he was an ok guy. He'd had miserable things happen in his life and I felt bad for him. I do remember thinking that he looked a bit worse than usual the last week he was alive. He wasn't making sense and seemed angry about it. I swear his beard looked much grayer than it had been days before, but maybe my mind invented it.

The last time I saw him, he took a drag from his cigarette, squinted and scanned the layout of the Pharmacy. "Fuck this place," he said, then stubbed out his cigarette and left.

He disappeared for a few days, then one evening his mother walked in. His mother is like a hundred years old, slouched over a walker, dressed in an ancient floor length fur coat, a mess of white hair piled on top of her head.

Jim and I were at the front counter. Jim had his arms crossed in front of him and was talking on and on. I was drinking weak coffee and staring off into space in front of me, daydreaming, ignoring the stream of consciousness flowing out of my boss.

Saint Peter's mom walked through the door with amplified effort and stared down at us from the top of the steps, leaning on her walker.

"Hi," Jim said to her, stopping his monologue and waving.

"Peter is dead." She replied.

My boss stared at her, blinking. He wasn't any good in situations like this.

"Oh, I'm so sorry. When?"

"Yesterday." She said. That was all she had to say about it. She turned around and pushed her way slowly back out the doors, the wheels on her walker squeaking, her fur coat dragging behind her.

I stopped at the bar after work to get a drink. Slow night—just a couple of people playing bar dice with the bartender. I stared down into my half empty glass of beer. "Shit, man," I thought, "this shit will kill you."

**The 2600 Block of Pierce**

The first half of my Pharmacy career and a short bit of time near the end was spent living in a neighborhood of Milwaukee called Riverwest, a place I love, in particular the 2600 block of North Pierce Street. I lived in four different houses on that single block.

Although I had visited the neighborhood a lot, I had at first lived on the East Side and then Bay View, before moving into a three-bedroom house on Pierce with two ravers I had met, Sleepy and 12 Ounce. More people moved in, Sleepy and 12 Ounce moved out and were replaced by more people until we averaged a flop house of about 5-6 roommates and usually someone passed out on the couch. I shared a room with my girlfriend at that time, Ruby, and she was the one who suggested I apply at the Pharmacy. I usually walked to work—just a block or so from my house was Saint Casimir Church on Bremen Street—similar in size and design to Saint Hedwig on Brady. Those were the two markers of my mile long hike to work and back, the noon bells of Saint Hedwig ringing out as I approached Brady and Humboldt.

I washed dishes at the Pharmacy for a few months, then I quit so me and Ruby could go backpacking through the United Kingdom and Ireland for the entire fall of 2000.

When we returned, we were a bit sick of each other, so we broke up. I moved directly across the street from my old house and got rehired at the Pharmacy as a cashier. I decided I wanted to take a trip to Australia, so I worked as much as I could—at the Pharmacy 12-8, had an hour off, and then worked down the street at a bar called the Hi Hat Garage as a doorman from 9 till bar close. I quit both jobs and took a trip to the West Coast and Australia for about 3 months.

When I returned, I got rehired at the Pharmacy again and moved into a house at the other end of the 2600 block of Pierce that was part of a complex of three houses called "The Barnyard." This was the wildest house on Pierce. Between the three houses there were a lot of drug and alcohol fueled parties and all the problems that went along with it. After a night of drinking around a backyard bonfire, I would often wake up to go to work and find someone passed out in the yard. The most notorious of these guys was "Loose Bruce," who was good company when he was sober, but turned into a complete ogre when he drank. He had been in prison in several states and his crazy behavior and violence are legendary to those who knew him to this day.

One time, another notorious character, Rusty, crawled through my bedroom window, completely blasted, and dug through a cigar box full of old cassettes I had found and began listening to and rewinding "Margaritaville" by Jimmy Buffet over and over, until I kicked him out. Like others I knew from these days, Loose Bruce and Rusty are no longer with us.

I moved off the block for a few years—I had gotten married, so the days of living in a house full of people for cheap rent and sacrificed sanity were over. But me and my wife moved to a house near the alley on the 2600 block, and that's where our relationship ended. Even though it was so long ago, it still gives me a pang of sadness when I walk by it. I hold my breath as if walking by a graveyard and try to keep my eyes on the sidewalk to avoid looking at it.

But despite that last chapter, I have so many good memories on that block—art and music and writing being created, partying with friends. It's where several neighbors decided to fly the pirate Jolly Roger flag outside their houses, and where a homemade miniature ice rink was created so people could play 2-on-2 hockey. The block is the command center of the Riverwest 24, a bicycle race that fills the neighborhood with non-stop bicycling, block parties, and strange bonus checkpoints. It's a block where I once saw a couple guys driving down the street on a motorized couch, saw an impromptu fire breathing show, and moshed in basement punk shows. One time I was walking home on a nearby block and passed a guy with huge, gauged ears with a snake sitting on his neck while he played the flute. That's so Riverwest!

It's a block where I fell in love and got into fights and had my heart broken. It's where I wrote some of my earliest published articles and found success and crushing defeat. I spent a lot of time sitting around backyard bonfires talking with friends, hanging out at bars like the Riverhorse and the Falcon Bowl—so much laughter—and got turned on to so much cool art, music, film, and writing. It's also where I heard horrifying stories of friends being victims of crime, learned about neighborhood sex predators, witnessed barroom blitzes and so much emotional pain—so many tears. Riverwest is a helluva place.

**Red Trips Da Light Fantastic**

My shift overlapped both the morning crew and the night crew, who began making the switch over around 2pm.

Second shift was much younger and weren't people who were going to be career waitresses. They didn't take their jobs seriously and as a result were much happier. Second shift was also usually a lot slower. I looked forward to it after the stressful first couple hours of my shift. The first shift waitresses would come up one by one and trade in their stacks of singles for twenty-dollar bills, and then they would leave as second shift drifted in.

Some of the second shift people I worked with were musician and poet Zack, the wonderfully sassy Abby, Podkayne, a film student, Tracy, a writer and actress, and Kelly and Gwen, sometimes referred to as the "Two-headed Party Monster." I loved chatting with Kelly and Gwen because they were young and into the local punk scene, so I got to live vicariously through them, listening to their stories about crazy wild basement shows they'd been to.

Several second shift people also worked weekend mornings. This is where Kelly and Gwen ran afoul of some of the first shift staff, because they sometimes showed up late and hungover from their basement show adventures. There was somewhat of a feud between the first shift and the Two-headed Party Monster. First shift said second shifters were lazy, sloppy, slackers, while second shift viewed first shifters as bitter, unpleasant old ladies who had been waiting tables too long.

Trust me, as cashier, I heard all about it from both sides.

When the coast was clear and first shift had left, Jim would burst out of his office behind the pharmacy desk as if released from a cage and head straight to a young waitress to make some terrible joke. He would sometimes sing and dance and he chatted with everyone in sight. He looked like he felt young, free from the wrath of first shift. Afternoon was his time to ignore bills, socialize, and then catch a nap at his desk.

The night crew had a dwindling number of regulars, but there were some. One group was a trio of old men who came in every evening for coffee—Phil, who almost never talked, unless it was a distasteful word or two of dismissal; Peppino, who only spoke Italian (his two companions, however, could not), and Red, who never stopped talking.

It was a terrible conversation dynamic. Red, as soon as he walked in the door, would talk continuously until (and while) he exited, in a voice loud enough for the entire building to hear in a thick Wisconsin (or 'sconnie) accent. He would stretch out the most mundane story—misplacing his keys ("day were in my pocket da whole time, fer cripes sake!"), noticing that a street sign had been replaced ("I said dat sign ain't da same one dat was der yesterday."), missing a TV show because he tuned into the wrong channel ("hey, dat ain't NBC I'm watching—it's FOX!")—into a long, anticlimactic tale.

Meanwhile, Phil would roll his eyes and occasionally croak out a couple words, usually "ahh, bullshit" and "ahh, c'mon," while Peppino would adjust his thick glasses, rub his forehead and mutter a long stream of something in Italian. Conversationally, they were three blind mice.

By this time I had started writing for local publications, and had a small digital audio recorder that I carried with me. I was so amused by Red's obnoxious storytelling, that on a few occasions I clandestinely recorded him when he hung around the front counter. Here's one of them.

Tea: What was that term you were using earlier? Something about the light fantastic?

Red: I tripped da light fantastic.

Tea: Yeah, that's it. I was trying to remember.

Red: You say "I tripped da light fantastic." Den dey're supposed to come back and say "Ya wanna gedda young lady? You dilly her in da dally, you twidder her in da twilight, then yer jackin in da dashcliffs in someone's underwear out on da washline, and den da grand finale, yer da phantom in da boudoir." Den you grab da guy's leg and go "sheep shanks!" (makes a grabbing gesture) You yell "sheep shanks!" (laughs) But yeah, "I tripped da light fantastic."

Phil: Ahhh, c'mon.

Peppino: [says something excitedly in Italian]

Tea: What? I don't get it. What does that mean?

Red: Oh, I don't know. It's just a term dat somebody...I told dat to da guy at da credit union, he said, I never heard dat before.

Phil: Ahh... ok, Red, see ya. You can stand here and bullshit all day.

Red: Or da one where I was on the treadmill. Da doc says, "we're gonna stop da treadmill and give you some dye, den you sit down for fifteen minutes, den we get you back on da treadmill." I say, "Doc, you ever hear da term 'heart dropsy?'" He says "nah, what is that?" I says "it's when a guy sits his ass down in a chair and he ain't got enough heart to pick it up again!" (laughs)

Tea: But what—

Phil: (in doorway) Hey Red, I'll see ya then if you're gonna stand here and bullshit all day.

Pepino: [asks question in Italian]

Red: Sheep shanks! (Exits)

Red of course, did what he did best—told a strange, rambling story that didn't answer my question in the slightest. Later, I consulted Google and found that "to trip the light fantastic" means "to dance nimbly or lightly" and was usually used in reference to ballroom dancing. Google, however, was no help in identifying Red's "dilly her in the dally" recital with the "sheep shanks" ending. That, I guess, was pure Red.

## Watt-ever

One of my favorite things about working at the Pharmacy was the constant flow of writers, journalists, musicians, performers, photographers, and artists of all stripes who circulated through the doors. The most creative people in the city stopped in to get a cup of coffee or a basket full of groceries and some used the lunch counter as their desk to write or sketch out their thoughts. I got a chance to talk to Michael Horne about his man-on-the-street reporting, watch as musician Paul Setser (RIP) wrote his setlist for his band's gig later that night, met actors, noise musicians, and film students.

The most notorious of them all was a guy who looked like a dirty Santa Claus (a role he actually portrayed in an annual XXX-Mas art show for several years), dressed in a fedora, white beard, sunglasses, and often sporting a fish tie—the former exterminator, poet, artist, and photographer named Bob Watt.

I was familiar with who and what Watt was. In the late 90s I was a contributor to an underground newspaper called the *Milwaukee Orbit*. At that time I thought my passion in life might be drawing comics, so I drew a comic strip for the paper called "Hella Gator" which was about the adventures of an alligator that loved to smoke weed. Bob Watt had a column that ran in the paper, along with his art. One of the *Orbit* editors, Trent, had told me all the stories about Watt.

One of the things Watt was most notorious for was his umm...dogged pursuit of artistically examining the female form or, to put it another way, soliciting young women to pose nude for him in his cluttered living room while he took photos on a point and click camera. He would cruise around the East Side in the Watt-mobile—a colorful car decorated with paintings, fake flowers and fruit, and hand out his business cards to ladies who caught his eye.

Right around the time I started working at the Pharmacy, Watt was gearing up for his 2000 campaign to run as mayor of Milwaukee. There was a Hooters restaurant downtown at the time, where he laid out his platform. Some of the points he campaigned on included moving the old County Stadium to the beachfront and turning it into a nudist colony instead of destroying it (it was instead demolished the next year) and a plan to build a motorized "masturbating machine" that would circle the UWM campus to service horny students who wanted to jump on for a ride. His campaign slogan was "Watt-ever."

One place Watt was not campaigning was in the Pharmacy's diner. Watt had managed a Pharmacy paradox—he was both a regular customer and, simultaneously, a *persona non grata*. He had been hanging around the diner, showing off his collection of nudes. He'd lay out photos of his naked models across a table like a set of tarot cards between the coffee cups and salt shakers, and a gaggle of old men would crowd around leering at the spread. Well, one day, the waitresses had made a stand and told Jim they wanted Watt permanently kicked out. No more old man peep show parties.

I understand where the waitresses were coming from. They had to deal with lots of day-to-day sexual harassment. They were ogled, propositioned, and sometimes even manhandled by old men (mostly) which had left them jaded and ready to attack against an unwanted shoulder rub or joke about Viagra. I remember walking through the cafe one day and witnessing a waitress drawing an invisible line above her cleavage with a hand angrily at an old goat who was staring deep into her bosom.

"You keep your eyes above this line when you're talking to me, got it?"

But the Pharmacy was also the source of where Watt's pictures were developed. We had a service that picked up film once a week, taking rolls of undeveloped film and replacing it with envelopes with the customer's pictures tucked inside.

We had about 5 wire baskets splitting the alphabet up and customers would come in and ask for their pictures by last name. The basket that included W was often overflowing with envelopes, and eventually was one of the few baskets that ever had pictures in it at all. Out of the corner of my eye, I'd look out the window and see the Watt-mobile pull up to the curb. Watt would slowly stroll in, pay for his pictures and make small talk with me while he stood to the side of the cash register, gazing at his treasures as he slowly flipped through them.

Between customers he would say, "Whaddaya think of this one? Not bad, huh?"

I'd look over to see him holding up a hazy photo of a young woman wearing nothing but a floppy sun hat, my eyes drawn to the un-airbrushed flesh, hypnotic areolas, and hairy puff of pubes. I'm certainly not offended by nudity nor mind seeing it, but being at work, it caused me some stress. I would slowly turn my head and see the waitresses staring daggers at me and Watt. They saw me as his pervert accomplice.

As the owner, Jim was in the middle of this conflict, and had brokered the odd "banned from the cafe, but not the front register" negotiation, terms the waitresses resented. They watched Watt like hawks, itching for him to cross a toe into their territory so they could attack.

One day, Watt was pushing his luck, in the eyes of the waitresses. He had been at the counter sorting his nude photos, when a curvy young woman strolled in and headed into the cafe. Watt's eye quickly appraised her swinging hips, and he eagerly followed her footsteps, reaching into his pocket and producing pocket lint and a business card. The angry look on the waitress's faces lit up—a-ha, got 'em! One of them dashed back to Jim's pharmacy counter, and a minute later Jim emerged, hands in pockets, and approached Watt, still chatting up his potential model.

"Nope. No. Got to go. Now!" Jim told Watt, his eyes scanning the floor. "Time to go. Not allowed in here anymore." Jim walked away, stopped at the counter and told me, "He's 69'd from here, don't let him back in."

"Ok," I replied. "But I think you mean 86'd."

Watt came up to the counter next. "He's as crazy as a bedbug," Watt said, pointing at Jim walking away. Then he adjusted his fish tie, gathered up his collection of nudes and strolled out the door.

Despite all that, Watt still patronized the Pharmacy instead of moving his business down the street to Walgreens. His friend Jon ran errands for him, including dropping off and picking up his film to be picked up. I knew it was Watt's film, because he would sometimes call and ask if the pictures were in yet.

I once stumbled upon where Watt found a new place to hold court—walking to the East Side, I had to pee, so I ducked into the McDonald's on North Avenue, and sure enough, there was Watt at a table full of old men, all hungrily feasting on McMuffins, coffee, and a spread of nude photos.

Watt died in 2012, age 86. I wrote a short obituary for him in the *Riverwest Currents* neighborhood newspaper. I talked to a couple of women who had posed nude for him when they were younger and they didn't have any regrets or anything bad to say about him. They wanted money, he wanted to take pictures of them naked. To some Bob Watt was a true artist, to others the ultimate dirty old man. It's a fine line, I guess.

**Opening Night**

The beginning of the end of the Pharmacy was Jim's decision to transform the back half of the store into a 40-seat theater. This was his dream—he no longer cared about the Brady Street Pharmacy business; it was boring. He wanted to be a great patron of the arts, and maybe even an artist himself. Selling hamburgers and cigarettes and newspapers couldn't compare to the allure of the spotlight. As such, he sunk a large sum of money to construct his own theater. He dreamed of edgy theater groups, ballet dancers, folk musicians, and screenings of classic and independent film.

The coolers full of beer, soda, frozen pizzas and TV dinners all went away, so did the section of greeting cards and the rows of canned goods, macaroni and cheese, and cereal—the Shredded Wheat was gone forever.

After this section of the store was cleared, with just the dingy grey carpet remaining, the construction began. There were months of jackhammering as the concrete floor was chipped away into tiered rows for seating, a wooden stage at the bottom of the pit. After months of dust and paint fumes, Jim's theater was done. As the finishing touches were being put in place, Jim pulled me aside one day and talked to me in an excited but hushed tone about his plan for opening night, which was to be a poetry reading. I can't remember who the poet was or what Jim thought his claim to fame was—he had been a poet laureate somewhere or belonged to some poetry foundation or some such. Whatever the credentials, Jim was very impressed.

"Keep this under your hat and don't tell your friends at the newspaper about this—I don't want word to get out," he said, overcome with the excitement of a packed house opening night. He didn't want to be in the awkward position of turning crowds of hundreds of disappointed people away if the event got too much publicity. In fact, he thought, better to keep it a secret. I had never heard of over-capacity poetry readings being a problem but thought he could perhaps be right—seating was limited to 40, after all, so I raised my eyebrows and my right hand.

"I shall not tell anyone," I swore to Jim.

Opening night rolled around. Jim had bought a popcorn machine for the theater, and I fired it up for the first time that night. The smell of buttered popcorn mixed with cigarette smoke and brewing coffee filled the air. The poet arrived. He looked the part, a rotund fellow with a white beard, holding a stack of sheets of paper. But few others had shown up. By ten minutes to show time Jim was pacing nervously, shock and fear written on his face—where was everyone? Why wasn't the theater packed? The audience totaled about six people, plus Jim.

I think this was the first inkling Jim got that the entertainment business was not going to be as easy or glitzy and glam-filled as he'd envisioned. It's a tough business that requires a lot of work and a lot of making the right connections—a role Jim, who hardly ever left the building, was going to struggle with.

That's not to say there weren't great or at least interesting productions that happened in the theater. But it was sometimes a nuisance. I remember one poor old woman was completely terrified—she was just picking up some cat food and other groceries and a theater group was practicing an upcoming "edgy" play that involved one of the characters screaming lots of profanity. Imagine you're thinking of cuddly Mr. Whiskers when you hear someone screaming violent threats about anal sex at the top of his lungs. Run for your life!

Over the years, I've felt Jim's pain. I've done successful events, but I've also just flat-out failed. The flop of a creative endeavor hurts. Why do I bother? Does anyone care? Why not just let the dream die?

It's quite harrowing to put blood, sweat, and tears into your art, only to have no one show up or show interest. Ouch. I wanna quit. I wanna never do anything like this again. I give up. This is why many creative people get discouraged and give up their craft. It takes a thick skin to pick yourself up, dust yourself off, and keep going. *It's my party and I'll cry if I want to.*

But Jim was stubborn. It was too late now, the theater had been built, at great expense. He would go down with the ship—the show must go on, as they say. Break a leg.

## You Can't Fight City Hall (but City Hall Might Stop by for Popcorn)

The theater, officially called the Astor Street Performing Arts Center, not only cost a lot of money to create, but was an ongoing money hole. Jim scrambled to figure out how to make ends meet and develop a stronger interest. He bought antique camera equipment and French movie posters to serve as decorations, tried to sponsor local film contests, and let experimental theater groups use the space for free.

Cash flowed down the drain, bills piled up, and Jim sought someone else to blame. He turned to the most classic scapegoat—politicians. The taxes were too high. The parking was bad. They didn't help the little guy, only the fat cats. It was their fault.

Jim began to write angry emails.

"Here, proof this for me," he told me one day, handing me a printout of a draft addressed to (then) Wisconsin Senator Herb Kohl. This was my cross to bear for Jim finding out I was a writer—he'd ask me to proofread everything he wrote as he was prone to spelling errors, grammar mix-ups, and severe problems with clarity.

One of the strangest things I've ever read was his script for a play he hoped would be performed in his theater. The play was only about fifteen pages long but had several anachronisms—early in the script we see a newsie out on a street corner hawking papers, yelling "Extra! Extra! Read all about it!" shouting about the day's headline about a new play opening. I assumed from this that the play was a period piece...but then a couple pages later a character is making a sexist joke about women watching too much *Sex in the City*. Did Jim still think newsies were walking around hawking the latest edition?

Later, when a character in the play, a reporter (presumably with a press card tucked in his fedora) is told by a play producer that actors and actresses drink too much, sometimes do drugs, and have promiscuous sex, the reporter yells, "hot damn, what a scoop!" and literally runs out the door to write up a page one story on this revelation.

Jim was stubborn and giving feedback or suggestions was futile—they went through one ear and out the other. So, when Jim asked for notes on the play, I just told him I wouldn't change a thing.

I read through the rambling screed to Senator Kohl. It made no sense to me, so I just circled his spelling errors and handed it back to him.

This was quickly followed by a draft of an angry tirade aimed at Mayor Tom Barrett, listing his woes of being a small business owner, stomped on by the boot of City Hall. This time Jim watched as I read it, hands on hips, face radiating defiance and anti-authoritarianism. I realized it was unreadable about a paragraph in, so pretended that I was reading the rest of it, moving my eyes back and forth, circling mistakes, and handed it back to him.

"Uh-huh." I told him.

"Oh boy! This is really going to shake up City Hall!" He told me and began strutting around the dingy grey carpet of the Pharmacy like Paul Revere.

\*\*\*

The next day I dragged myself into work. Jim was waiting up front by the cash register, his arms folded in front of him, waiting for me.

"Do you remember that email I sent off to city hall?!" He said, giddy with himself.

"Yes." I replied.

"No response from them, the cowards!" He told me.

"Well, it's only been a day," I replied, but he ignored me and gave an impromptu speech to the customers in line at the cash register about the story of David and Goliath, and how City Hall just ignored the Good People of the City of Milwaukee.

\*\*\*

The next day Jim saw me come in and almost ran down the aisle to the counter.

"No reply! I guess I was too much for them to handle…with a hey nonny nonny and a ha cha cha!" Jim randomly broke into song and dance sometimes, and he started doing an awkward version of the Charleston.

\*\*\*

The day after that, I walked into work and Jim was talking to some little old ladies who were regulars. They could hardly see or hear, but he was telling them about how he was like Jimmy Stewart's character in *Mr. Smith Goes to Washington*, his unanswered email was proof that City Hall was shaking at its foundation.

"Otherwise, they'd respond to my email! I sent it right to the mayor himself!" Jim told them proudly.

"What?!" Asked one of the little old ladies.

In the afternoon, it was slow and typical for Jim to lean back in his chair at the pharmacy counter, fold his hands behind his head, and doze off into dreamland until a phone call or customer startled him out of sleep. This particular afternoon he was snoozing away, and I was slapping mouthwash and packages of cookies with a price gun up at the front counter. I heard the front door open and turned to see who the customer was. I smiled.

"Mayor Barrett!" I said. He shook my hand.

"I'm looking for Jim," he said. "I got an email from him."

"He's at his desk back there," I said, pointing to the pharmacy counter. I watched attentively as the Mayor walked back to Jim's desk, and not seeing anyone, called out, "Hello?"

Talk about a rude awakening! Jim jumped to his feet, his hair sticking up in an Alfalfa sprout, bleary eyed. I will never forget that look of shock on his face…was he still dreaming? Was he hallucinating? Nope, he was face-to-face with the Mayor himself.

I don't know what they talked about. Jim folded his arms in front of him and nodded politely. Then Jim talked for a while, the Mayor shook his hand and bought a bag of popcorn on his way out. Jim sat behind his counter and didn't show his face for the rest of the afternoon, but later slowly strolled up to the front counter.

"So how about that, the Mayor responded to your email in person?" I prodded, seeing if he might share their discussion. But Jim just replied, "Yeah," took the big bills and credit card slips out of the register and walked back toward his desk.

For once he was out of things to say.

**Anvil Chorus**

One day, I walked into the Pharmacy and found an unusual scene—more so than typical. Music was blaring uncomfortably loud, blasting through the building—it was opera, the type Bugs Bunny might bonk his victims on the head to with a big mallet. The song was "Coro di Zingari," in English "Anvil Chorus," from the opera *Il trovatore* by Giuseppe Verdi.

I scanned the room—a handful of customers looked just as confused as I was. The waitresses looked like they were about to murder someone. Mo was chuckling, smoke spilling out of her mouth between laughs as she watched my dumbstruck expression.

I walked over to her by the counter.

"Mo, what the—" But she held up her hand as she ashed her cigarette.

"He got some new speakers for his stupid fucking theater and he's showing them off like a kid," Mo said. I could barely hear her over the Anvil Chorus. "But we got a bigger problem. If you want any money today, you better grab your paycheck and haul ass down to the check cashing place, hon. They started calling the bank to see if there's enough money before they'll cash our checks."

A quiet panic crept into my gut—NO MONEY. Mo saw the look on my face.

"Go," she said. "I got it covered. Besides, you're early today for once."

"Be back soon," I said loudly. I started walking toward the Pharmacy desk. Jim was standing behind the counter, his hands resting behind his head as he stared off into space smiling slightly, soaking in the rousing operatic anvil strikes. He saw me walking towards him, shuffled through a small stack of paychecks, licked a finger, pulled mine out and slapped it onto the counter top.

"New speakers!" He said loudly as I approached.

"Alright!" I yelled back. The current predicament made me not want to kill time. "Loud!" I said, then beelined to the backdoor, folding my check along the perforated edge. I hadn't even had time to take my coat off, so I stuck the check in the inner pocket, next to a packet of gum and some pens. The sound of the Anvil Chorus faded behind me as the door closed and I stepped into the cold, spring air. I exhaled, my condensed breath blasting out in a cloud as I quickly walked east toward the check cashing place, a few blocks away.

All of the employees had started making this same trek on payday because our checks kept getting bounced, messing up our bank accounts. Most of the employees were living paycheck to paycheck. I certainly was, so a bounced check would overdraft my account and I would be broke until it got fixed. It was an annoying hassle, so we had started cashing the checks and letting Jim deal with the aftermath when they bounced. But now this well had also run dry.

I crossed Brady and Humboldt as the bells of Saint Hedwig began to ring their loud declaration that it was noon. Half a block later I heard a car horn tapping out a signal, and my brain shook. Anvils, church bells, car horns! How was I going to pay my overdue rent? I looked and saw one of the waitresses, Kim, and her brother Bobby, who was one of the cooks, driving Kim's rusted out minivan, still honking the horn. She rolled down the window and leaned out.

"We're going to beat you there, motherfucker!" She laughed, tossing her cigarette butt to the curb. I shrugged and threw my hands up, like "what are ya going to do?"

When I turned to look at the minivan, I saw a figure on the sidewalk behind me, and I swiveled more to get a better look at who was tailing me and saw that one of the dishwashers, Cesar, paycheck in hand, had just left out the back door of the Pharmacy. I got an adrenaline surge—fight or flight, money or no monies.

"Next on *The Amazing Race*," I said in my best TV announcer voice. "Who will cash in their check first?" I began whistling Anvil Chorus loudly as I picked up the pace, an old lady waiting at the bus stop eyed me suspiciously.

It was Friday, so when I arrived I found two long lines behind the open windows. It was a mass of people who had just gotten paid, waiting to approach the bulletproof glass windows, sign their checks with a pen attached to a beaded metal rope, then slip them into the sill underneath the window. In exchange they'd get their cash, pay their electric bill, buy stamps and bus passes. I could see Kim and Bobby toward the beginning of the line. They were called up to a window. There was some discussion with the teller, but I couldn't hear what was being said over the loudmouth at the window next to them. Time ticked on.

*Ah shit*, I thought. *It's taking way too long. The money isn't there.* Suddenly, Kim turned around and scanned the room. She saw Cesar in line behind her, then her eyes found me. "Tea, Cesar, better come up here," she announced. We approached the bench.

"I'm sorry y'all, but we just called the bank and they don't have the funds for your checks. None of them," the woman behind the bulletproof glass said. "If money clears you can come back on Monday." Kim's face was red with anger. Bobby sighed, rolled his eyes and said "shit." Cesar scanned the dirty linoleum floor below him. I was in a small panic but kept a poker face, or so I imagined. The four of us pushed our way out the door.

"You guys want a ride?" Kim asked us out on the sidewalk.

"Nah, I'll just walk," I said.

"I know, what's the hurry, right?" My coworkers got in the van, I stuck my hands in my pockets and strolled west, my head filled with bad thoughts and budget math that wasn't adding up.

When I got back to the Pharmacy, I found Jim was flustered and talking to a couple of the waitresses. He had been confronted by them—hell no, they wanted their money NOW! After much heated negotiation, Jim agreed he'd pay half of the employees' paychecks in cash on the spot, and pay out the other half on Monday, hopefully making enough cash over the weekend to get by.

I stuffed the money in my pocket, then heard one of the cooks, Gary, call out to me. He asked if I wanted to join the rest of the diner staff in throwing a couple dollars in to buy lottery tickets.

"Why not?" I said and threw a few bucks onto a pile of singles and fives in the kitchen's windowsill. Gary started asking everyone what they were going to do once we won and became millionaires.

"Oh you know, buy my girlfriend a bikini and head for a tropical island," I said, but I said that because I was trying to fit in and be normal. Really what I'd do with that money is buy a creepy, old house and fill it with creepy, old books. Other people mentioned elaborate vacations and dream houses.

"I'm going to buy this place with my money." Kim said.

"Jim won't sell," Gary responded.

"Oh, he'll have to after I hire a team of fancy lawyers to go after his ass. The Health Department alone will shut this place down."

"So, you're going to buy it, and what, rename the place Kim's Diner and be the boss," Gary laughed as he flipped a burger onto a bun dressed with lettuce and tomato.

"Hell no. I'm going to tear this fucking place down and build a parking garage here in its place," Kim said, angrily stubbing out a cigarette so she could go check on her tables.

**Note to Mo**

I quit the Pharmacy in 2009. Some of my friends worked for a company downtown where you would transcribe phone calls for people that were hearing impaired. There were cubicles as far as the eye could see. It was boring, repetitive, annoying—but there was no fear of having to race co-workers down the street to cash a paycheck or having to deal with kicking someone out that was having a full mental breakdown. I didn't miss the Pharmacy so much as I missed some of my co-workers, so I resolved to stop in regularly to get breakfast and other necessities once in a while. I found a letter in one of my old notebooks. I must have re-written it because I remembered stopping in and finding that Mo was home ill, then thumbtacking the note on the bulletin board behind the cash register. This draft read:

Mo—
Well, the new job is going OK. It's a bit sterile, but it's on the 12th floor, so it has a nice view of downtown. It certainly lacks the "unique character" of the Pharmacy though.

I will be stopping in mornings, at least once or twice a week to get bus tickets (if there are any) and breakfast (if there is any food).

It's been a wild ride, Mo. Thanks for all you've done for me. If you ever need anything, give me a call. In the words of Jim, "Done!"

Xoxo

Tea

Shortly after that, I helped Mo move. Her landlord was selling her Polish flat and she was forced to move to a 19-story apartment building run by the Housing Authority named Riverview, right off of Brady. We had to move her furniture to the 8th floor via elevator. While we waited, Mo told me about the place, which was available only to seniors and disabled adults—it sounded like a senior citizen prison, where different cliques had carved out turf. The old Russian ladies hung out in the laundry room all day, gossiping in Russian and eating stale bread. The elderly black residents hung out in the courtyard. Different cliques vied for control of the TV room. Mo mostly hid out in her apartment with her cats.

After that, I fell out of touch with Mo, and stopped by the Pharmacy less than I thought I would. I was busy with the new job and working on trying to figure out how to be a writer. I had just started working on my first book. I do remember having a drink on Brady Street one night and walking by the Pharmacy. It was late, bar close, and the lights were out, the diner empty and silent. I sighed. *This place.*

But I did get one last phone call from Mo. It was the phone call to let me know that the Brady Street Pharmacy was finally dead.

**Lights Out**

Here's what I remember from that phone call from Mo. Jim had gotten himself into a shockingly dumb, crazy bad financial situation. The Glorioso Brothers store across the street needed to expand, they had more business than they could handle. Cannoli sales were up. They had heard that the Pharmacy was circling the drain and approached Jim with an offer. Jim agreed and asked for $10,000 in earnest money as a deposit, which he promptly spent trying to get some stock on the empty store shelves. Then he reneged on the deal. He apparently borrowed another $10,000 from a shrewd developer to repay the Gloriosos, but they didn't want the money and refused it. They wanted the building and they sued.

Jim had another, more immediate problem—he couldn't pay his bills. The shelves were mostly bare—he owed every distributor money and his attempt to spread stock out thinner just made the shelves look even more empty. They stopped delivering newspapers. Jim would drive down the street and buy a few copies of the paper, then resell them to his customers for 0% profit just so they'd have something to read over breakfast. That cover story on *People* magazine was yesterday's news...or rather news from 3 months ago, as his magazine distributor had also cut him off. Then they stopped picking up the garbage, so he would stack bags in the garage until he had time to go to the dump. There were vermin.

The bill that finally killed the Pharmacy was the one from the energy company. He owed them an astronomical amount and when they called to tell him they were about to turn off his power, Mo told me that in the heat of the situation he made a threat of suicide. The energy company called the police, who showed up and chased him around the building. They eventually caught him and booked him. Then the energy company shut off the power.

The staff, in the dark and without a boss, thanked the regulars who happened to be there for their years of patronage. When they had cleared out, Karen (the only waitress with a key) locked the doors, leaving the cafe dark and disheveled, unbused tables and half-empty coffee pots, frozen in that moment. The employees all caravanned over to the Baker's Square restaurant, to sit down together and enjoy being served lunch for once instead of serving it. That was the last staff gathering of the Brady Street Pharmacy.

And that was it for the Pharmacy. The End. Jim decided to sell to the Glorioso Brothers after all—he really had no choice, the lawsuit was dismissed, he moved out and the keys were handed over. I heard whispers about him over the years—the last I had heard he was running the pharmacy department of a big box chain.

This is what I can tell you about the Brady Street Pharmacy—there won't ever be a place quite like it ever again, it was the last of its kind in Milwaukee. The beloved Oriental Drugs, a similar pharmacy counter, store, and diner on the corner of North and Farwell Avenues next to the beautiful Oriental Theater, closed in 1995 (many of the regulars and a couple of the employees migrated to the Pharmacy). Goldmann's Department Store, an eccentric maze of clothes and household goods and weird junk with a triple horseshoe of lunch counters closed in 2007—it had been open for 111 years. Hayek's Pharmacy, a corner store and pharmacy counter shuttered in 2018 after 100 years of business.

Some independent establishments that contain an element of these places still remain—you can get cheap greasy food along with a window seat view of the city at Ma Fisher's ("an East Side tradition since 1932") or Miss Katie's Diner downtown, as well as a handful of other independent spots around town, shop at a time capsule gift store at the 90-plus-year-old Winkie's in Whitefish Bay, and frequent the newer coffeehouses like Rochambo and Brewed Cafe on Brady Street, HiFi Cafe in Bay View, and the Anodyne cafes in Bay View and Walker's Point, to name just a few. But these places are quickly vanishing too, and the pandemic of 2020 only twisted the knife on the already tough challenge of maintaining a small business.

It's an incredible sadness to think about these unique places being lost—they were neighborhood community centers, social spaces that offered something Starbucks and Walgreens and Wal-Mart can't replace.

My memory of the Brady Street world I was a part of is already fading. I took a walk down Brady Street recently and found that some things were exactly the same, others had changed quite a bit. I struggled to see what it used to look like—my brain stalled as I stared at an ugly new condo building, eventually I was able to visualize the laundromat that used to stand there. I guess that's why I wanted to write these stories down, before they are gone forever.

After I quit, after it closed, people would ask me, "Do you miss the Pharmacy?"

"Not yet," I'd respond. I still had some raw feelings about everything I had experienced. "Ask me again in ten years."

Well, it has been ten years now.

I do miss it.

**About the Author**

Tea Krulos is the author of five other non-fiction books—*Heroes in the Night*, *Monster Hunters*, *Apocalypse Any Day Now*, *Wisconsin Legends & Lore*, and *American Madness*. He lives and freelances in Milwaukee for publications like *Milwaukee Magazine* and *Shepherd Express*. An article he wrote for *Milwaukee Magazine* won a 2020 Excellence in Journalism Award from the Milwaukee Press Club. His book *American Madness* won a National Indie Excellence Book Award. He writes a column (with a tie-in podcast) called "Tea's Weird Week" at his website, teakrulos.com.